DATE DUE

ELK

Tom Jackson

Grolier
an imprint of

www.scholastic.com/librarypublishing

Published 2008 by Grolier
An imprint of Scholastic Library Publishing
Old Sherman Turnpike, Danbury,
Connecticut 06816

For The Brown Reference Group plc
Project Editor: Jolyon Goddard
Copy-editors: Lesley Ellis, Lisa Hughes,
     Wendy Horobin
Picture Researcher: Clare Newman
Designers: Jeni Child, Lynne Ross,
     Sarah Williams
Managing Editor: Bridget Giles

Volume ISBN-13: 978-0-7172-6223-6
Volume ISBN-10: 0-7172-6223-5

**Library of Congress
Cataloging-in-Publication Data**

Nature's children. Set 1.
     p. cm.
Includes index.
ISBN-13: 978-0-7172-8080-3
ISBN-10: 0-7172-8080-2
1. Animals--Encyclopedias, Juvenile.
QL49.N38 2007
590--dc22

                    2007018358

Printed and bound in China

PICTURE CREDITS

Front Cover: Shutterstock: Wesley Aston.

Back Cover: Nature PL: Mangelsen, Tom;
Shutterstock: Robert Kelsey; Superstock:
Age Fotostock, Mark Newman.

Alamy: Franzfoto.com 22, David Hosking
28; **Corbis**: Richard Hamilton Smith 21,
D. Robert and Lorri Franz 44; **FLPA**: David
Hosking 9; **Nature PL**: Niall Benvie 40;
Shutterstock: Wesley Aston 5, 18, Vera
Bogaerts 14, 32, Nathan B. Dappen 26–27,
Christa DeRidder 35, Ronnie Howard 2–3,
13, 36, Denis Pepin 17, Mike Rogal 6, Victoria
Short 10, Brian Wathen 31; **Still Pictures**:
Bios Auteurs Mord 4, 43, H. Brehm 47;
Superstock: Tom Murphy 39.

Contents

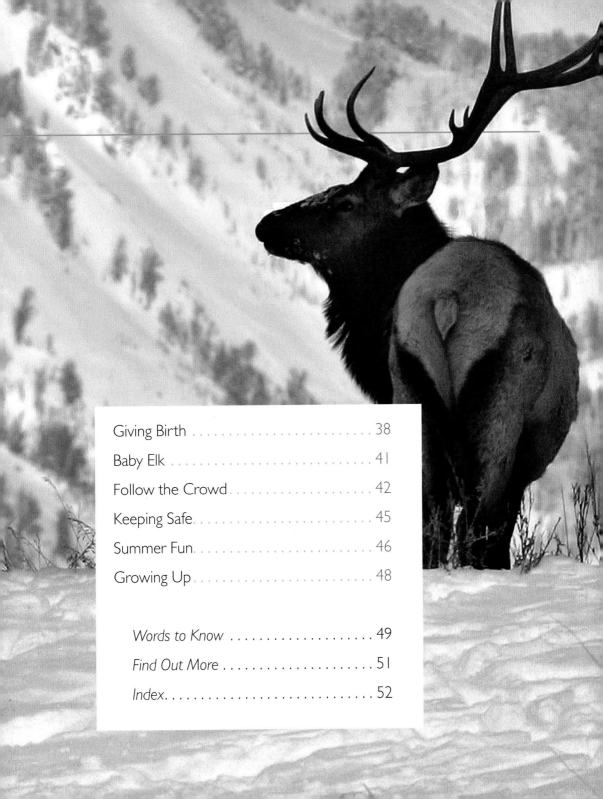

FACT FILE: Elk

Class	Mammals (Mammalia)
Order	Cloven-hoofed mammals (Artiodactyla)
Family	Deer (Cervidae)
Genus	*Cervus*
Species	Elk (*Cervus canadensis*)
World distribution	North America, Europe, and Asia
Habitat	Prairies (grassland), meadows, and woodlands
Distinctive physical characteristics	Males have long antlers that branch in many places; the coat is brown with a paler rump; in winter the deer grow a mane
Habits	Elk move around in a herd; they are mostly active in the early morning and in the evening; elk migrate each year
Diet	Grasses, shrubs, twigs, and bark

Introduction

The elk is one of the largest types of deer in North America. Elk also live around the world in places such as Scandinavia and Siberia. But speaking to someone from Europe or Asia about elk can get confusing. That is because people from different places call elk by different names. Scientists call elk by the old Native American name *wapiti*. In Norway and Russia, people use the word "elk" when they're talking about the moose! As you can imagine, it can get very complicated!

This adult male elk, or stag, has huge antlers.

A white-tailed stag looks a lot like its bigger cousin the elk. Both live in North America.

Elk Family

Elk belong to the family of **mammals** called the Cervidae (SIR-VI-DAY). This family contains all of the world's deer. Other deer living in North America include moose, caribou (reindeer), and white-tailed deer.

Deer of all kinds share several physical features. For example, elk and other deer have four toes on each foot, but only walk on the front two toes, which form a split **hoof**. Deer have no top front teeth. They use their tongue to grasp foliage, which they then cut with their bottom incisors, or front teeth. The adult males, or **stags**, of most **species** of deer grow **antlers** each year. The females, or **hinds**, of some types of deer have them, too.

The body of a deer is long and graceful. They also have slender legs, a long, pointed face, and a short tail. Like their cousins the antelope, deer can run fast to escape **predators**.

Big Beast

Elk are big animals. Few other deer grow to
a larger size. In North America, only the moose
is larger—and the moose is the largest deer
of all. An elk stag is about 8 feet (2.5 m) long.
It can weigh more than 1,000 pounds (500 kg).
Elk hinds are smaller and lighter than the stags.

Though they are long and heavy, fully grown
elk do not grow very tall. Their shoulders are
about 4 feet (125 cm) above the ground.
However, the deer's head and antlers are
always held high. That can make the animal
seem twice as tall!

A stag and hind greet each other. The hind is smaller and does not grow antlers.

9

An elk stag rests in
a woodland clearing.

Habitats

Elk live in two **habitats**, or types of places. In summer they live in the open, feeding in grassy meadows. There is plenty of food in summer. In winter it is too cold for the deer to live out in the open. Deep snow makes it harder for elk to move around and escape from danger. In winter, elk move to areas of woodland, protected from the snow and wind.

In the past, elk ranged across much of North America, from the Allegheny Mountains westward. Today farms and towns cover lands that were once elk habitats. Elk currently live in wild areas that have stayed unchanged. Most elk live in the Rocky Mountains. There are meadows on the high slopes and woodlands in the valleys. Each fall, elk come down from the meadows to the woodlands below. They make the return journey, back in the open meadows, each spring. These long journeys between the elk's summer and winter homes are called **migrations**.

Pale Patch

Elk have a pale patch of fur on their backside, or rump. The Shawnee, a Native American people, named the deer *wapiti*. That means "white rump." Elk are still often called *wapiti*, especially in western North America and also by scientists.

The rump fur is not really white. But its lighter color stands out against the rest of the deer's darker coat. Zoologists, or people who study animals, are uncertain why elk have this patch. The patches may help the deer recognize each other when moving in a herd. Or they might help attract mates.

Unlike its cousin the red deer, the elk's coat changes color with the seasons and its habitat. In winter, it is lighter and more gray in color. That changes to a dark reddish color in summer. Zoologists once thought that red deer and elk were the same species. Tests have now shown that they are different animals.

An elk has a
pale patch of
fur surrounding
its tail.

13

In summer an elk's coat is dark red, which clearly shows the white patch around its tail.

Changing Coats

The thickness of an elk's coat changes throughout the year to suit the weather. In summer the coat is made of a single layer of short hairs. The hairs are stiff and glossy. That is all the elk needs in the hot weather. A thicker coat would make the elk too warm.

In summer the hairs covering the body, face, neck, and legs are a dark reddish brown. The tail and its surrounding patch are pale brown or yellow.

The summer coat is too thin for winter. In fall the hairs of the summer coat fall out. The fur is gradually replaced with a much thicker winter coat. This process is called **molting**. The elk also molts in spring, when the winter coat is replaced by the summer coat.

Winter Warmer

Elk live in some pretty chilly places. So their winter coat has to keep them warm and dry. The winter coat is fully grown by the end of September. Unlike the summer fur, the winter coat is made up of two layers. The lower layer, or **underfur**, has many thin and short hairs packed tightly together. They act as a cozy blanket wrapped around the deer. The outer layer is made up of longer and thicker hairs called **guard hairs**. These hairs work much like a raincoat does. They stop rain and snow from making the underfur wet.

The winter coat makes the elk look a bit different. It is more gray than the summer fur. The thick fur also makes the deer look larger than it does in summer. The fur is thickest around the neck, where it grows into a shaggy mane. Though hinds grow manes, they are not as long as the stags' manes. The stags use their manes to impress the hinds.

An elk's winter
coat is thickest
around the neck.

17

A thick skull and strong neck support the weight of a stag's heavy antlers.

Amazing Antlers

Like all male deer, an adult male elk, or stag, has antlers. They rise from his head like a spiky crown. It is no wonder that the elk is sometimes called the "king of the mountains." The elk's antlers weigh between 40 and 50 pounds (18 and 23 kg). That's about the weight of an average-sized six-year-old child.

You would probably find it a struggle to lift someone that heavy off the floor. Imagine walking around carrying that weight on your head! Male elk have to carry that weight for several months each year. Their antlers can also grow up to 4 feet (1.3 m) long. The Irish elk, which no longer exists, had the biggest antlers of any animal—they measured 13 feet (4 m) across!

Every year in late winter, the elk's antlers fall off and a new set grows back in early summer. The antlers are covered with a soft skin called **velvet**, which rubs off as the antlers grow and turn to bone.

New Antlers

Elk lose their antlers in February. The place where the antlers join the head gradually weakens. Eventually, the weight of each antler is too much. The antler falls off with a loud crack. Both antlers rarely fall off at the same time. Most stags will have to spend a week or so with the weight on their head unbalanced until the remaining antler falls off.

The fallen antlers leave a stump of bone on each side of the stag's head. The stumps soon begin to grow into a new pair of antlers. Antlers are made of bone, but they are soft and flexible as they grow. The velvet covering the growing antlers contains blood vessels that feed the new antlers.

Above this elk's eye is the stump left after an antler has fallen off.

In late summer the velvet outer layer of a stag's antlers peels off.

Rubbed Away

By the middle of summer, an elk's antlers are fully grown. They become completely hard. The velvet is no longer needed and it dries up. That makes a stag's antlers itch. He rubs his new antlers against bushes and tree trunks. The velvet peels off to reveal the shiny bone underneath. The fresh bone is white at first but gradually darkens to brown.

The stag's antlers are now ready for the rut. During this period of fighting in fall, stags compete with one another for hinds.

Antler Ages

You can tell how old an elk stag is by "reading" his antlers. As the deer gets older, his antlers grow bigger. Each year the antlers are longer and they have more branches, or **tines**. An elk with antlers that are just a simple spike is one year old. A two-year-old stag has three or four tines on each of his antlers. By the time the stag is four, it has six points on each antler. At that time the antlers are about 4 feet long (1.3 m). From this age, the antlers do not grow longer or develop any more tines. They do, however, become thicker and even heavier as the stag gets older.

Antlers reach their maximum size when the stag is eight or nine years old. After that, the stag is too old to grow such large antlers. An older stag's antlers get thinner each year and grow fewer points.

On the Hoof

Like all hoofed animals, elk are built for a life on the move. The elk's hard hooves are made from a hard material called keratin. Your fingernails and toenails are also made of keratin. The hooves protect the elk's feet from sharp stones on rough ground. But they are also useful for walking on soft mud and snow. The hoof is divided into two parts, which helps distribute, or spread out, the elk's weight, stopping the hoof from sinking into soft ground.

Elk tend to walk most of the time. But they can run when they need to. Their long legs are built for powering the deer at high speed. Elk can run at 30 miles an hour (48 km/h) for short distances. That is very fast for an animal that weighs half a ton. Elk are also excellent swimmers. Long legs make elk good jumpers, too. The deer can make running jumps over 6-feet- (1.8 m) tall fences.

The underfur of elk keeps them warm even in the coldest weather.

A stag uses a back hoof to scratch its velvet-covered antlers.

A Day in the Life

Elk are often on the move in the early morning or in the evening. The rest of the day is spent feeding or resting. Elk groom themselves by scratching and licking their coat to remove bugs and dirt. The deer can reach most parts of their body with a hoof or its mouth. For example, they scratch behind their ears with a hind hoof.

Elk like to spend the night in a high area. From there, they can see or smell danger coming. Elk are not fussy about where they sleep. They do not make a bed. They just lie down wherever there is room. Elk do not sleep the whole night through. Instead they take several short naps, waking up now and then to take a lookout. One member of the herd always stays awake while the others sleep.

Feeding Time

Elk eat a lot—more than 20 pounds (9 kg) of food a day if they can find it. What elk eat depends on the time of year. In winter elk often go hungry for long periods because the deer cannot find enough to eat.

In summer elk eat grass and other leafy plants that grow close to the ground. They also enjoy a tasty flower or mushroom. In winter their food is buried under snow. Elk try to dig the snow away with their hooves. Or they look for hillsides where the wind has blown the snow away. But for most of winter, elk have to make do with less tasty food. Most elk survive winter by eating twigs, bark, and even pine needles.

In summer and fall elk eat a lot of grass and other meadow plants.

When an elk lies down, it's usually chewing the cud.

Double Chew

Can you imagine going to school after a breakfast of twigs? That meal is not going to make you feel full or give you the healthful nutrients you need. Elk face this problem on a daily basis. Even grass, their favorite food, does not have a lot of nutrients. That is why elk have to eat so much—to make sure they get all the nutrients they need.

Elk, like all deer, have a large stomach with four separate chambers. After being chewed and swallowed, an elk's food enters the first stomach chamber. There, the food is mixed with stomach juices that begin to digest the food, or break it down. After a little while, when the elk is resting, this food moves back up the throat and into the mouth. The elk then chews the food again, grinding it up even more. This process is called chewing the **cud**. The cud—a paste—then returns to the stomach and moves into the next chamber for further digestion.

Herds and Bands

Elk do not live in families, with a mother, father, and their children. They live in a larger group called a herd. In summer the stags and hinds live in separate herds. Stags live in small groups called bands. The hinds live in larger groups. A group of hinds also includes the **calves** that are still growing. In fall a single stag joins each group of hinds. He fights any other stag that tries to join the group. This stag also makes sure that the hinds do not wander off and join another group. The stag **mates** with all the hinds before winter arrives.

When winter comes, it is time to migrate to the woodlands. Several small herds gather into a single large herd. This herd may contain as many as 100 stags, hinds, and calves. The stags are tired after fighting for mates. So a hind takes charge of the herd, leading it to the wintering ground.

Elk gather in big herds in their winter woodland home.

A stag bugles. This loud call impresses the hinds and scares away other stags.

Noisy Deer

Deer are not known for making many noises. But elk are actually very noisy. When an elk is frightened, it makes a snorting sound called a bark. The bark warns other deer that danger is near. During the **mating season**, stags make a loud call known as a **bugle**. Bugling is a way for the stags to show off. If the call is very loud other males are too scared to challenge them.

Calves squeal to their mothers when they are hungry or frightened. Different notes and loudness of call mean different things. Regardless, the mother hind is always there to look after her youngster.

Giving Birth

Hinds give birth in May and June. When the baby is due, the hind leaves the herd and looks for a quiet place, safe from predators. The hind gives birth away from other elk so she can have some time alone with her new calf. That helps the hind and calf learn each other's smells and sounds.

Most hinds give birth to a single calf each year, although some have twins. Newborn elk weigh between 30 and 40 pounds (13 and 18 kg). That is about five times heavier than the average weight of a newborn human baby. The calf has reddish brown fur like its parents. It also has large pale spots on its back.

A newborn calf is unsteady on its feet.

A calf reaches
under its mother
for some milk.

40

Baby Elk

After her calf is born, a hind licks her baby until it is clean and dry. Within two hours of being born, the calf can stand up. But it is too shaky to walk far. However, once the calf is on its legs it can **nurse** on its mother's milk and is soon gaining strength. Within a few days, the calf can follow its mother. Within a week, the calf is running around with the other youngsters in the herd.

The calf takes its first bite of grass after a few weeks. But the calf continues to nurse for the rest of summer. As fall arrives the calf will finally stop nursing. Then, its mother prepares to mate again.

Follow the Crowd

Elk calves can walk and run about a week
after they're born. But they still cannot travel
as fast as most adult elk. The mothers band
together with their calves. The hinds make
sure that the group does not travel too fast
for the youngest calves.

The calves enjoy life in the herd. While the
adults are resting or chewing the cud, the calves
play chasing games. The youngsters have mock,
or pretend, fights. Sometimes the calves toss
sticks into the air. A few hinds take turns looking
after all the calves in the herd. This allows the
other mothers to go off to graze.

Elk calves have spots on their back. These markings disappear as the calves get older.

43

A stag charges
at an intruder.

Keeping Safe

Healthy adult elk are generally safe from attack, even from big predators such as cougars, wolves, and bears. The deer can defend themselves with jabs from their antlers or powerful kicks. Elk can also run away to safety. Predators generally go for sick or older elk that cannot get away. But predators also attack elk herds when the new calves arrive. Bobcats, coyotes, and even golden eagles prey on baby elk. It is up to the mothers to keep their young safe.

A calf is never far from its mother. If the mother hears her baby squeal in fright, she instantly runs to protect it. If she spots danger, she barks a warning to the calf. The young elk immediately drops to the ground. Its spotted fur acts as camouflage, helping it blend into its grassy surroundings.

Summer Fun

Adult elk are usually calm animals. They do not spend time playing games. The adults leave that to their calves. Elk calves are at their most playful in summer. Then, they are just a few months old. One of their favorite things is playing in water. Such play is not just great fun. It also keeps the calves cool and helps them grow strong running muscles. As the calves play, their mothers watch calmly from the riverbank.

The young deer splash through the shallows and take cooling dips in the deeper water. The calves make the most of their playtime. At summer's end the calves and their parents have to make a difficult journey, or migration, to the herd's wintering ground.

A playful elk calf runs in a stream.

47

Growing Up

Elk calves stay close to their mother for an entire year. They remain together during winter. In spring it is time for the pair to separate. They usually separate just after the mother gives birth to a new calf. She then drives her older offspring away.

At the age of one year, the young elk can look after itself. Even so, the calf will not become an adult for a few more years. Hinds are fully grown at the age of three. At that age they begin to have calves of their own. Three-year-old stags are old enough to mate. But they are not big enough to compete with older males for hinds. Most stags do not become fathers until they are at least five years old. Elk can live for about 15 years.

Words to Know

Antlers   Bony hornlike projections grown by male elk. Antlers fall off in winter and regrow the following summer.

Bugle   A loud call made by elk stags.

Calves   Young elk.

Cud   Swallowed food that is brought back into the mouth for chewing a second time.

Guard hairs   Long, coarse hairs that make up the outer layer of an elk's coat.

Habitats   Types of places where animals live.

Hinds   Female elk.

Hooves   The feet of sheep, deer, and many other animals. Hooves are like giant, thickened fingernails or claws.

Mammals	Animals that have hair or fur and feed their young with milk.
Mates	Comes together to produce young.
Mating season	The time of year when animals mate.
Molting	Shedding fur and growing new fur, usually at a change of season.
Nurse	To drink milk from a mother's body.
Predators	Animals that hunt other animals.
Species	The scientific word for animals of the same type that mate together.
Stag	A male elk.
Tines	Pointed branches of an antler.
Underfur	A thick layer of short hairs that covers the skin.
Velvet	Soft skin that covers growing antlers.

Find Out More

Books

Furtman, M. *Seasons of the Elk*. Northword Wildlife
Series. Minnetonka, Minnesota: Northword Press, 1997.

Hodge, D. *Deer, Moose, Elk, and Caribou*. Kids Can Press
Wildlife Series. Tonawanda, New York: Kids Can Press,
Ltd., 1999.

Web sites

Elk (Wapiti)
www.enchantedlearning.com/subjects/mammals/deer/
Elkprintout.shtml
Facts about the elk with a picture to print and color in.

Pennsylvania Elk Herd
www.pennsylvaniaelkherd.com/elk00021.html
Information about Rocky Mountain elk.

Index